Cheetahs

Cheetahs

Jenny Markert

THE CHILD'S WORLD®, INC.

Published in the United States of America by The Child's World®, Inc.
PO Box 326
Chanhassen, MN 55317-0326
800-599-READ
www.childsworld.com

Product Manager Mary Berendes
Editor Katherine Stevenson
Designer Mary Berendes
Contributor Bob Temple

Photo Credits
© 1996 Anup Shah/Dembinsky Photo Assoc. Inc.: 30
© 2001 Art Wolfe/Stone: 16
© Daniel J. Cox/naturalexposures.com: 2, 19, 23, 24, 26
© 1992 Fritz Polking/Dembinsky Photo Assoc. Inc.: 15
© 1996 Fritz Polking/Dembinsky Photo Assoc. Inc.: 20
© Joe McDonald/www.hoothollow.com: 9, 29
© 1995 Kevin Schafer: 10
© 1996 Kevin Schafer: 13
© 2001 Manoj Shah/Stone: cover
© Tom & Pat Leeson, The National Audubon Society Collection/Photo Researchers: 6

Library of Congress Cataloging-in-Publication Data
Markert, Jenny.
Cheetahs / by Jenny Markert.
p. cm.
Includes index.
ISBN 1-56766-884-4 (library bound : alk. paper)
1. Cheetah—Juvenile literature. [1. Cheetah.]   I. Title.
QL737.C23 M363 2001
599.75'9—dc21
00-010768

On the cover...

Front cover: This female cheetah lives in the Masai Mara Game Reserve in Kenya.
Page 2: This adult cheetah is resting in the Masai Mara Reserve.

Table of Contents

The African plains are quiet in the late afternoon sun. A herd of gazelles calmly munches on tall grass. Little do they know that another animal is watching them! Crouched low in the nearby grass, a big cat moves slowly toward them. Once the cat is close enough, its streaks out of the grass. The startled gazelles scatter in every direction, trying to escape this fast animal. What is this big cat? It's a cheetah!

What Are Cheetahs?

Cheetahs are cats. They are also **mammals,** which means that they have hair and feed their babies milk from their bodies. Cheetahs are taller and slimmer than other big cats such as lions and tigers. Cheetahs can't roar like other big cats, but they can purr like a small house cat. They can also yelp like a dog!

This adult cheetah is getting a drink on a hot afternoon in Kenya. ⇒

Cheetahs have long, thin bodies with four long legs. They have an arched back and a long tail, too. Their long tail helps them keep their balance as they turn quickly while chasing other animals. The food animals they chase are called their **prey.**

How Fast Are Cheetahs?

Cheetahs are the fastest animals on land. They can run up to 60 miles per hour—as fast as a car on the freeway! Despite their speed, cheetahs don't always catch their prey. A cheetah can chase an animal for only a couple of minutes before getting tired. If the prey animal dodges and runs long enough, the cheetah gives up the chase.

This female cheetah is chasing a gazelle ⇒ she has picked out from the herd.

What Are Cheetahs' Claws Like?

Cheetahs' claws are different from other cats' claws. Other cats can pull their claws back into their paws. This keeps the claws razor sharp, so the cats can climb trees and defend themselves. Cheetahs can't pull in their claws. Instead of being sharp and pointed, the cheetah's claws are dull.

Cheetahs can't climb tall trees or defend themselves as well as cats with sharp claws. But the cheetah's claws are very good for running! They stick into the ground like the spikes on a football player's shoes. That keeps the cheetah from slipping as it runs.

Cheetahs like this one sometimes climb short trees. This female's ⇒ dull claws would not help her climb anything much taller.

Cheetahs are **carnivores,** which means that they eat other animals. They find weak or sick animals the easiest to catch. Most wild cats hunt at night, but cheetahs hunt during the day. They usually hunt alone, but sometimes two cheetahs hunt together and share a meal.

When a cheetah is hungry, it looks for a likely prey animal. Then it crouches low in the grass and waits. The spots on its fur help keep other animals from seeing it. This protective coloring is called **camouflage.**

⇐   The cheetah in this picture is difficult to see as it
waits for prey in some tall South African grass.

The cheetah remains low in the grass. Very slowly, it sneaks toward its unsuspecting prey. When it is close enough, the cheetah darts out and runs after the prey. Some prey animals are fast enough to get away. Other animals are no match for the cheetah's speed.

Here you can see an adult cheetah as it chases a gazelle. ⇒

On the plains of Africa, cheetahs find lots of different animals to eat. They prefer medium-sized animals such as antelope, impalas, and gazelles. They also eat smaller hares and ground birds. Sometimes, however, cheetahs hunt bigger animals such as zebras.

⇐ Cheetahs like this one often kill large prey by holding it by the throat. Since it can't breathe, the animal soon dies.

Usually, a cheetah eats its meal right where the animal falls. The cheetah isn't strong enough to drag a large animal to a safer eating place. When the cheetah eats out in the open, other animals such as lions, leopards, and hyenas can see the cheetah's fresh meal. The cheetah must gulp down its food before the other animals arrive. Often, other animals attack the cheetah to steal its food. If the cheetah doesn't eat quickly enough, it must leave hungry. Then it rests for a while and hunts again.

This female has started eating the gazelle she killed. ⇒

A female cheetah usually has three to five babies, or **cubs,** at a time. This group of babies is called a **litter.** Cheetah cubs can be born anytime during the year. The mother gives birth in a safe place hidden from enemies. The young cheetahs have a silver tuft of hair called a **mane** over their heads and backs. Scientists think the mane helps protect the cubs. From a distance, the cubs look like *ratels,* tough-skinned, smelly animals that aren't good to eat.

⇐ This young cub lives on the Serengeti Plain in Kenya.

Very young cheetah cubs sleep a lot and drink only their mother's milk. As they grow bigger, they start walking and following their mother. They spend most of their time biting, pushing, and chasing each other. This play-fighting makes them strong and able to defend themselves.

The mother teaches the cubs how to hunt. First, she brings them a dead animal. The cubs watch her eat and copy her. Later, the mother cheetah knocks down an animal but doesn't kill it. She calls her cubs so they can learn how to kill it. Finally, the cubs must catch their own dinner.

⇐ Here a young mother is dragging a gazelle over to her cubs.

Do Cheetahs Have Enemies?

Lions sometimes kill cheetahs if given the chance. Eagles also like to carry off cheetah cubs that aren't with their mothers. But for the most part, cheetahs have few enemies in the wild. Instead, their biggest enemy is people. People are using more and more of the cheetahs' living space, or **habitat,** for farming and building. As a result, the number of cheetahs is dropping.

This cheetah mother and her cubs are watching nearby ⇒
animals in the Masai Mara Game Reserve in Kenya.

People also kill the animals cheetahs hunt for food. In some countries, laws have been set up to protect cheetahs. Many zoos have also started raising cheetahs in hopes of returning them to the wild. If we find ways to protect these fascinating animals, there will always be cheetahs racing across the African plains.

Glossary

camouflage (KAM-oo-flahj)
Camouflage is coloring that helps an animal hide or blend in with its surroundings. The cheetah's spots act as camouflage.

carnivores (KAR-nih-vorz)
Carnivores are animals that eat only meat. Cheetahs are carnivores.

cubs (kubz)
Baby cheetahs are called cubs. Cheetah cubs learn how to hunt from their mother.

habitat (HAB-ih-tat)
An animal's habitat is the type of environment in which it lives. People have destroyed much of the cheetah's habitat.

litter (LIH-ter)
A litter is a group of babies born to an animal at one time. A litter of cheetahs usually has four babies.

mammals (MAM-mullz)
Mammals are animals that have hair, are warm-blooded, and feed their babies milk from their bodies. Cheetahs are mammals, and so are people.

mane (MANE)
A mane is an area of long hair around an animal's head. Baby cheetahs have a silver mane on their heads and backs.

prey (PRAY)
Animals that are killed and eaten by other animals are called prey. Cheetahs catch their prey by running very fast.

Web Sites

http://www.pbs.org/wnet/nature/cheetahs/

http://www.CheetahSpot.com/

http://www.africat.org/ (Be sure to click on "Predators in Africa.")

Index